The Complete Petrosexual

A handbook of style for the modern dog

By Sterling Sugar Magnolia
As told to Nola Thacker

stewart tabori & chang

New York

Published in 2005 by
Stewart, Tabori & Chang
115 West 18th Street
New York, NY 10011
www.abramsbooks.com

ISBN: 1-58479-433-X

Created by Paint Chip Productions
Publisher Ellen Stamper
Design by Kathie Davis of Davis Design
Art Direction by Pauline Foster
Production Management by Toni Gardner and Lisa Bartlett
Dog Stylist Shiffra Steele

The text of this book was composed in
Sans Serif, Simoncini Garamond, and Colleen.

Printed in China

10 9 8 7 6 5 4 3 2 1

First Printing

Stewart, Tabori & Chang is a subsidiary of
LA MARTINIÈRE

...Can you say
"fashion
victim"?

Contents

Introduction

I was born lucky. Even as a puppy, I was a classic example of bull terrier beauty. My dear mother taught my siblings and me from the day we were born how to interact with people. Our human, a bull terrier breeder with extremely strict standards about who would have one of the puppies of her beloved and carefully bred bull terrier kennels, subjected potential puppy families to rigorous interviews and those that did not meet the highest standard were rejected.

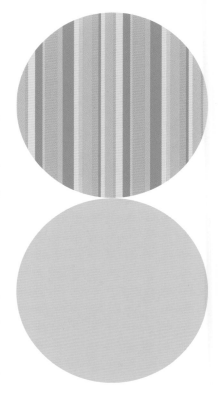

Thus at the tender age of 7 ½ weeks I found myself in possession of a very worthy human, and while I was of course sad to leave my mother and littermates, I was glad to be able to add the human to the list of those held in the closest affection of my heart.

I took up residence in a large city in a most dog friendly neighborhood, with several lovely shops full of dog food and canine accoutrements; a clean, well-lighted veterinary practice staffed by thorough, well-trained doctors; flanked by a park that welcomed dogs off-leash before 9:00 a.m. as long as the dogs and their humans were well behaved; and countless restaurants where the words "doggie bag" guaranteed delightful morsels upon my human's return home.

I have traveled extensively, sniffing the smells of many ports, as it were. And while I discovered early on (and with, I admit, a shock) that bull terriers were merely one group of the vastly varied and almost infinitely adaptable canine species, it only dawned on me gradually that not all the human companions of dogs are worthy of sharing the same sidewalk.

I also noticed, as I walked through my fair city, that even with trainable humans, many dogs were ferociously failing to be the best that they could be. On all sides, dogs paraded mismatched leash and collar sets, little shirts with cute sayings, cuts that not even a mother could love, matching dog and human outfits suitable only for the annual Halloween festivities. How could this be? Was it possible that the canine citizens of our mighty metropolis could be so clueless? Apparently so.

It was then that I realized that there was more to life then guiding my human through it, more than snoozes in the sun at a sidewalk café while she ate off a menu that one hoped would include doggie bag worthy items, more than a walk in the park.

I rolled up my sleeves (metaphorically, of course—rolled-up sleeves are appropriate only in limited situations) and went to work. And that is how the idea of the petrosexual was born.

...Feathers are not for every dog

chapter one

Choosing
One's Owner

your fate is in your paws

In order to fulfill your inner dog, reach your full potential and be the dog about town you were meant to be, you must make the all-important first step: choosing the correct owner.

Think about it. Do you, a border collie or Australian cattle dog, who much prefers to spend your boundless energy clumping sheep or corralling cattle, wish to spend your life with suburban mom and dad and assorted smaller bipeds, fresh from a viewing of say, *Babe*, who think you should be able to expend your instincts and energies in a house and garden situation?

No. You will grow so frustrated you will uproot the garden, carve toothy designs on all available furniture legs and be ceaselessly scolded for your inability to curb the instinctive and therefore almost totally irresistible urge to nip pants legs and diaper bottoms in an effort to corral or clump the family.

Your family of poor choice will become angry. You will become increasingly unhappy. If your people are particularly beastly or stupid, they will tie you outside most of the time or keep you kenneled with only short strolls to take care of business.

Or they might take you to the nearest shelter, where your fate, my dear, could well be to go to the big kennel the sky. Which at that point, alas, might even seem welcome to you. This is not the way for the pet-rosexual to go.

...Layabouts and couch potatoes need not apply.

You might well ask how can you, a mere puppy, possibly make a choice when it seems to be the human who is in charge of the "Choose-One-From-Column-A" department. True, a responsible breeder will make the proper choice for you. But if you are unfortunate enough to hail from the pet shop window, as so many of our poor brethren do, or have already reached the shelter situation, you will have to do everything you can.

If you are a small, not particularly energetic dog, such as a pug or similar mix, look for a quiet older individual or stylish young male couple who appreciate the appearance of a small distinctive dog that prefers to receive visitors rather than make visits. If you are a border collie type (and you know who you are) or a Jack Russell the Ripper and need to play or you'll go completely mad, focus on the active sort, someone who looks as if they know how to exercise even if they don't know dogs (and honestly, would they be shopping in a pet store if they had a clue?)

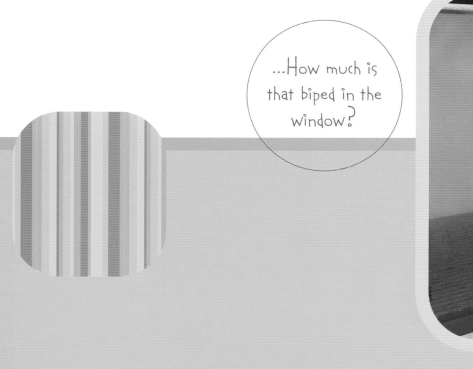

...How much is that biped in the window?

Smart dogs, foolish choices.

If you're a pug, Maltese or other small and cuddly type, say no to: marathoners; mountaineers; surfers (well, let's just make all the athletically inclined bipeds); large families with very active children; apartment dwellers above the first floor in non-elevator buildings; any family with very active dogs. Say yes to: retired persons (on substantial incomes at good addresses, naturally—doorman buildings preferred); ladies who lunch; ladies and gentlemen who shop (at the best stores); single individuals given to sedentary activities such as brooding and reclining (freelance editors and writers are good, as long as they have enough work to support you); anyone who calls you princess.

If you are a rottweiler, ridgeback; Staffordshire terrier; bull terrier or pit bull terrier, avoid: people who look as if they have a chip on their shoulder which they might like to express in such illegal activities as dog fighting; first time dog owners (they will be extremely difficult for you to train if they don't know what they are doing); sedentary types; and those who look humorless or anal retentive; and anyone who murmurs about "protection." Say yes to: people who love your breed and are familiar with it; hikers, runners, and tennis players; families with older children in them who are accustomed to dogs; and, surprisingly, single women who are soft on high maintenance dogs.

...Small breeds should aspire up...Princess perhaps?

Laboradors, Golden retrievers, and like mixes should avoid the obvious biped deadbeats who would not give any dog, animal or significant other a good home; then focus on what interests you: families with children for you to romp with? Go awww factor to the tenth power; hiker? Fine. Owner of sailboat or other watercraft? Excellent. Multi-dog situation? If it works for you! You are adaptable creatures, and I salute you.

So, how do you choose the correct person for a happily ever after?

First, remember that education begins at first impression. Let's say you're with a prospective male human at shelter or shop. You race toward him. You lick his shining shoes. If he seems unfazed by this, squat and cop a pee. If that also fails to move him to shrieks and urgs, well, friend, he definitely has potential.

If, on the other hand, he goes all judgmental on you for doing what comes naturally, back away slowly. Avoid eye contact. Allow the other, less informed puppies to fawn and wriggle. If necessary, cower away. This person is not for you.

...A well-aimed pee will weed out the overly squeamish and the intolerant.

Nor are people who think it is cute when their children hold puppies upside down or squeeze the life out them; adoring parents who find it sweet when their tippy toddler pulls the ears, tails or any other appendage; anyone who thinks they'd just like that nice big bruiser over there for protection; and, oh, yes, anyone who can't get off their cell phone long enough to really get to know you in situ.

In fact, these are not good choices for any dogs, but that is another book.

Where was I? Oh, yes, chances are the above Mr. and Mrs. Wrongs are going to be far too busy to spend any time with you at all—and whose fault will it be when you aren't a "good dog"? I think we know the answer to that. Can you say hello shelter, here I come? You did not choose wisely.

...Avoid excessive cell phone users, appendage pullers, anyone looking for a dog for protection.

But say you've spotted a human with dog-owning snaps and the shelter has erupted in chaos around you. To your left, Max the Mix is doing amazing back flips off the walls of his kennel. To your right, Lolly the Lab is demonstrating that yes, she can climb chain link. This is where you must dare to be different.

Do not bark! Do not under any circumstances turn back flips. It's all in the hips. Wag. Hard. The whole adorable posterior should be in motion.

Get that tail up! Go yogic with the motions.

Now, move in for your close-up. Press your darling muzzle to the kennel gate and stare up into your prospective owner's face adoringly. Play bow and stand up again.

Repeat.

Only utter a small "look-at-me" yip when eye-contact is made, flatten your ears a little and put that backfield into motion! Then, when the attention is focused on you, drop into a sit. Raise your paw imploringly. You have just tapped into what I call the awww factor. Remember that term.

...awww factor

Once you've made the break from litter and/or shelter you will be able to employ the A factor in many useful ways.

"Awww," they say, right on cue then the door opens for a meet and greet.

...The adoring gaze makes bipeds go weak in the knees.

> ...Adoptions work both ways — you should be interviewing the human as much as he is interviewing you.

The awww factor: Steps to closing the deal

do:
1) wag
2) adore
3) bow
4) sit
5) paw

don't:
1) bark
2) backflip
3) crotch-dive

Now, this is very important.

Do not dive nose-first into the person's crotch. A crotch check (dog version) is useful for determining many key items (if only humans knew), but now is not the time. Concentrate instead on cementing how right you are for one another. If a trial walk is involved, try not to pull too hard on the leash or spin too many circles of joy. Instead, stop as you stroll to look lovingly over your shoulder. You are saying, "Isn't this fun?" "Shouldn't we do this together every day of our lives?" As you continue to interview the person, listen closely to the conversation between your potential new roommate and the breeder, pet shop clerk, or shelter attendant.

Bad questions: "Do I have to train her?" "Will she be much trouble?" "Do you think she's messy?" At this point, pee directly onto his shoes. Good questions: "Where do you recommend we go for training?" "I sometimes work long hours—can you recommend a dog walker for those times?" "Does she like any special food?"

Then go for it. This one is definitely trainable, possible, and ownable. Do what you must. Work it. Let him know that he deserves only the finest and you are it. If you have chosen well, a future of warm beds, real liver treats, gourmet dog biscuits, and lovely plates of leftovers await you. You will teach this lucky human the joy of long walks in the park, of the importance of stopping to smell the flowers (and garbage), playing hide the bone, and chase the Frisbee and how to sleep in the sun, splash through the puddles, and enjoy a nice roll in the grass. If you do your job right, your person has so much ahead of him, if only he knew. As do you. Your fate is in your paws.

...A big smile always seems to seal the deal.

chapter two

Beds
and Doghouses

location, location, location

Well, well. So you are the chosen one. And you've chosen wisely.

Let's discuss habitat. If you are in an apartment, chances are your person will want to keep you in an indoor kennel for short stretches of time—at least until you've worked out the house training and what-to-chew rules. With regard to housetraining, you will soon have him house-trained. He will be taking you out for walks three times a day because he has realized that he doesn't want you going poo on his floor, carpet, shoes, or any other interior surface.

Once you've got him straightened out on that, gently guide him into real estate. Like where you are going to sleep.

As in, not on the floor. Humans operate under the quaint notion that we like to lie around on floors. Darling, please. The petrosexual does not sleep on the floor.

...Do not under any circumstances allow your human to think it is okay for you to sleep on the floor.

You must, I repeat, must have a throne. Select a chair, a sofa or a bed and make it your own. You will know you have succeeded when you and the uninformed visitor hear these words: "Oh, don't sit there, that's Buffy's chair." Be gracious as you jump up on your chair and the unfortunate visitor slinks toward the sofa, trying to laugh it off.

...Visitors must always know who rules the roost.

Dog Beds

Next, you need to decide whether you will require a dog bed or human bed for your nighttime beauty sleep. Well, before you reject dog beds out of paw, take a look at what is available.

Darling, they come in lovely faux sheepskin. Plush velour. Heated, treated, and yes, ruffle-pleated. You can catch your Zs on orthopedic foam or eiderdown. Make cute little squeaking noises in your dreams (you do, you know) while curled on real velvet. Peer adorably out from a bed emblazoned with your initials.

And this is your bed. You do not have to share it with anyone else.

...The perfect bed if you are called princess... or want to be.

Humans can be just a wee bit annoying in bed. They sprawl, they snore, they hog the covers given half a chance, and if you sleep at the foot of the bed, they've been known, horrifying but true, to kick a sleeping dog.

Not for nothing do we say, "Let sleeping dogs lie."

Let me strongly suggest that should you choose to have a dog bed of your own, you have it put in the bedroom with your person. Otherwise, your person might fail to see the logic of you having your own chair in the living area.

Dog bed or human bed?
Ask yourself these questions:

Does your human snore?

Toss?

Steal the covers?

Sprawl?

Yes to any of these leads me to suggest you go with your own bed.

Are your answers no, no, no, and no? Then dive in. Burrow under the covers. It's nice, isn't it? Humans are just so sweet when they're sleeping. Aren't they?

...Animal prints are highly chic and a great way to update a classic bed...so long as they're not from a real animal.

...If your taste runs to timeless modern, you'll love this bed.

...If you crave the comfort of a human bed without the flailing limbs of the accompanying human, then this is the bed for you.

...If you chafe at the confinement of a bed frame but like to be up off the ground, your own personal ottoman will work well—or you may simply appropriate your biped's.

Doghouses

Oh, dear, he went and did it. He let himself go on the internet. Or maybe she foolishly fell for a frivolous fold out in House & Garden. Perhaps he ordered one of those igloo things from a catalog or built one from a kit—complete with adorable little window boxes beneath painted-on windows. And you got a custom doghouse.

Did you ask for a dog house in the family garden? Did you say, oh, yes, I'd much rather sleep outside? No, you did not. You must make it clear that you want to sleep IN THE HOUSE. Once you have established that, you can condescend to nap in the doghouse. Be gracious. After all, if humans can have second homes, why can't you? Of course, it would have been so much nicer if it came with a heated floor.

A doghouse with a climate control is always nice. But in terms of architectural style, I prefer something simple and classic—Craftsman or Cape Cod perhaps. A plain, solid house with a nice paint job can never be wrong. However, if you've been saddled with the likes of castle turrets or Victorian gingerbread, you might be able to tone it down with a little discreet chewing.

But if your person goes for tromp l'oeil, what are you going to do? At least hold out for original interior artwork featuring themes dear to a dog's heart, say, bones with wings, or a flattering portrait of *vous*, or literary scenes featuring famous dogs.

Keep in mind, too, that first of all you're colorblind and secondly it's not as if you actually live there (this last point is key).

And remember: Doghouses also offer shelter when you are, well, in the dog house. Misunderstandings invariably arise between species thrown into close contact, unfortunately one dog's chew toy can be another human being's Manolos. When it is best to lay low, and under the bed doesn't do it for you, having a little retreat, snug and waterproof, has merit.

...You say Manolo, I say chew toy.

For example: Your human is holding something recently savored by you aloft. Her mouth is opening and closing and there is the tell-tale furrow between the brows. Do not try to reason with her. Do not try to charm her. The awww factor is not going to work, at least not right away. Tuck your tail between your legs and head for the doghouse. Having unearthed a nice bone, you can settle in until your human sees the light of reason.

After all, how were you to know that the leather belt wasn't left on the floor just for you? Didn't your own dear mother bring things to the den just for you and your littermates to chew? Every dog knows that whatever hits the floor is fair game—but sadly, alas, every human does not.

...Tucking your tail between your legs is the only method of training your biped to forgive those unfortunate interspecies mishaps. After all, canines are the diplomats of the animal world.

Wait, and look repentant and your human will come to you. Allow her to coax you from the doghouse and back into the house. Accept the peace offering, preferably something in liver or pork, graciously. Snuggle up and offer a lick or two.

And remember—try not to do it again, whatever it is because dog-houses really are much more fun as little second homes than as permanent residences. Aren't they?

Diet
and Exercise

you can teach an old human new tricks

chapter three

The "D" word—yes, diet.

You are what you eat, Pudgy. And don't you forget it. For those over-sized bags of discount kibble from the big box store, one big word:

No. The petrosexual is far more dis-criminating.

I mean, you don't buy your clothes there, do you? Who knows how long that stuff has been sitting on the shelf? Nutritionally complete? Well, sure it is. But read the ingredient list. I mean, purified chicken feathers? What is that? And what does dried beet pulp have to do with the price of chopped liver?

But honey, my money is on the kibble like the stuff I saw being pushed at a dog show. The sales rep was actually crunching up bits of it to show how wholesome it was.

...There is no "Big and Tall" department at the pet store.

27

And let's do a little cost to poop ratio here. Cheap kibble means more filler. Filler, frankly, goes in one end and comes out the other. So what your human saves on kibble, they're going to shell out in pooper scooping.

But kibble is only the base of the dog food pyramid. The petrosexual understands that the true objects of desire are much, much higher on the food chain. Oh, I don't mean sirloin steak—at least not every day. Milk bones have their place, after all. But even better—homemade peanut butter dog cookies.

Your human isn't handy in the kitchen? And no upmarket pet supply store is just around the corner? Did I teach you nothing about location?

...Chew sticks are great for carrying or, well, chewing

Get your human to work the internet. Point and click, dear. In no time at all, you'll be chomping carob chews, pigging out on pig ears (oh oink, oh rapture), downing dainty mint biscuits...

...When eating, don't gulp as if you were a drain backing up.

Human food?

Too divine. Too easy to overindulge. And a portly puppy is not a pretty puppy. So try to limit your intake. Be selective. A bit of cheese here, a morsel of ham there is really all you need.

And just say NO to chocolate. Chocolate is, alas, fatal for some dogs. Yes, it is true, dear reader. Chocolate can kill. And you never know which dog it will strike or what the fatal quantity could be—possibly as little as one toxic truffle. So don't go Godiva into that good night. There's plenty to eat without chocolate. Trust me.

...There are so many excellent gourmet dog foods, you probably won't miss human food, particularly if your human's culinary skills are sub-standard.

That said, let us now come to the artfully stuffed bone or toy. All dogs do it.

I personally have gnawed away many lovely hours en kennel with a plain bone stuffed with peanut butter or cheese.

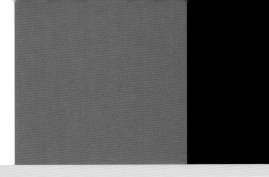

...In good pet shops treats are often placed tantalizingly close to our noses.

Know Your Dog Treats

Perhaps this bone was even hollowed out by lucky you. Although some humans get all squeamish over raw marrow bones, I feel a nice big bone is a most appropriate palate pleaser from time to time. I don't mean chicken bones or other nasty little throat-sticking, stomach puncturing twigs, but a proper beef marrow bone. If you fear mad cow disease (although corgis and cattle dogs swear all cows are mad) then by all means, go organic. Frankly, it's what I do.

...Freshly baked biscuits and rawhide chews are two of life's simple pleasures.

Toys such as the divine hard rubber variety also lend themselves to being stuffed with hot dogs, biscuits and yes, more peanut butter or cheese. It's my personal favorite. So send your owner out to play without you from time to time. It's good for him. And you get to stay home and be king of the castle.

While we're on the subject of treats, training, and fine dining, do try to train your person to keep the toilet seat down and the lid closed. Not only is this a courtesy that humans should extend to one another (but alas, frequently do not)—it is a hygienic necessity. Simply put this means:

Don't drink from the toilet. Yes, I know. It seems such a, shall we say waste that every home in the entire country is equipped with a nice, large constantly replenished drinking bowl along with a (usually) male biped who makes it readily available. But fellow canines of good taste—No! In the first place, this is not a big porcelain dog dish, this is a human toilet. You do not drink or dine where you take care of business, do you? Certainly not. And you would be repulsed if you saw your biped doing the same. Likewise, your biped is (one hopes) repulsed when he sees you slurping in his bathroom—particularly if you were to lick his face directly afterward.

Exercise

Now that we have established that diet is not a four letter word, let us move on to what humans quaintly call "exercise." Humans like exercise. They bend themselves into all kinds of shapes that dogs can do naturally. Therefore, dogs do not need to do aerobics, weight lifting, cross training, or yoga. Although a little person-and-dog yoga session never hurt anybody. Peace, ohm, and dog biscuits.

But let's move on to the real objects of meditation and desire. Let's talk tennis balls: little, yellow, delicious. Fetch is a perfect game for tennis balls that humans seem to particularly enjoy and since many dogs excel at it (don't get all smug, you retrievers out there—you can't help yourselves and you know it), you should encourage the behavior in your human. This is a good thing. It is important to exercise your human regularly.

...Can these toys survive a Jack Russell?

...Rubber ball? Never.

...Tennis ball? Only if you like fuzz on your carpet.

...Hard rubber toy? We have a winner!

Up goes the ball, up you go. You make the catch, nothing fancy. You return the ball to the human. The human is overjoyed. See how simple it is?

And it is not limited to tennis balls. The L.L. Bean sort of dog who loves the great outdoors can use the rustic stick—be it on mountain-side or urban park. The Barishnidog can express himself best with the Frisbee. Almost any toy is fetchworthy.

Masters of the game can add spice by pretending not to see where the ball went. When you do "find" it, you are a genius! A gooooood boy! A smart girl! "Gooooood human!" You might want to woof back. "Smart biped! Now throw it again!"

...Almost any toy is fetchworthy.

...It's important to exercise your human regularly.

But the most important exercise, particularly for the apartment dog, is the walk. Also known as "walkies" and W-A-L-K. As if you didn't learn how to spell that right away.

Walks require you to attach your human to you with a leash. You want the leash and collar to be suitable to the job, a subject I cover more thoroughly in chapter four called Your Fashion Pedigree. (see page 40).

Words every dog should know how to spell.

- *walk*
- *eat*
- *out*
- *treat*
- *vet*
- *shots*
- *dinner*

...Carrying your own leash shows a sense of mastery and control. We know who's the boss in this relationship!.

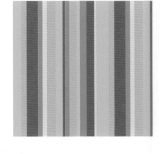

If you live in an elevator building and are a large dog, remain calm while riding the elevator. Smile benignly. If the occasion warrants, offer your paw. You cannot build up too much good will, especially if you are of a Schwarzendogger build.

...Large build dogs must always behave extra well so as not to intimidate those around them.

If you are a small dog, the trip down in the elevator, across the lobby floor and around a block or two may be more than sufficient for your needs. If you're a big dog, or almost any type of terrier, you will want more.

Perhaps you can persuade your person to take up jogging. It keeps your human healthier and happier and once you've trained her to jog in place while you perform essential sniff tests, you will find it is the beginning of a beautiful ritual.

The walk is also good for patrolling your territory. After all, leaving your calling card on hydrants and lamp posts is what it's all about, isn't it? (And girls, don't tell me you don't do it, too. I know you do.)

The walk can also lead to the dog park, where you can sniff face (and more) with other dogs.

...We canines are naturally able to create amusing games using any available object.

Sit your person on a bench inside the fenced in area set aside especially for dogs. Try to make sure she is near another compatible looking human. Then feel free to indulge yourself in chasing, leaping, barking, rolling, and yes, roughhousing.

Pretend you are *très fierce.* Growl and yip. If toys are banned in the dog run, find a nice stick, and try to make the other dogs jealous with it by barking, "Look, look! I have a stick and you do not. And it is an amazing stick. The best stick."

...Size matters.

But pay attention to dog park manners. If another dog bares his or her teeth at you and does not want to play sniff or engage in a best stick competition, do not persist. When a dog says no, a dog means no. And be kind to the puppies. After all, you were a puppy once yourself.

Even if you are dog who does not like to get his feet wet, you may find you like the water. (And all you Labradors out there, no rude remarks. Not every dog is Esther Williams. For some a little tiptoe through the tidal pools is more than enough).

Does your person have a boat? Lucky you. Not only do you get to acquire a neat little form-fitting life jacket, but you also get to indulge in the marine equivalent of riding with your head out the window (something frowned on by humans, but let that pass). Just make sure you don't go dog overboard.

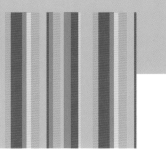

...Even if you don't like the water, raincoats are not a fashion forward substitute for life vests... no matter how cute the coat.

37

On the shore, you can play chase the waves, try water fetch, or teach children, if you have them, how to really dig a hole in the sand. Do not, however, make the mistake of burying anything in the sand. Wet sand makes everything smell alike—and finding what you've buried extremely difficult.

Feel free to bark at the seagulls. Discretely check out the high-tide line for dead fish—they rate off the smell meter.

When you've finished patrolling the waterfront, try a nice nap in the sun (sunscreen for those dogs with thin fur and pink skin showing through—doggie sunburn hurts), or take a snooze in the shade of a beach umbrella.

And drink plenty of water but not the salty kind. You'll need it. Insist your human not head for the beach without it.

Best Beach Activities:

- *looking for dead fish*
- *teaching children to dig holes*
- *napping*
- *checking out other hind legs*

...A trip to the beach is no excuse for dressing like a cartoon character.

Swimming pool among your assets? Less interesting, but it's not without it's uses. If the pool has steps, wade right in. Be careful though. If the pool doesn't have steps and you jump in, you won't have a way out—unless you can climb a ladder. You could end up floating à la *Sunset Boulevard.* No steps? Claim a chaise, and don't forget the sunscreen.

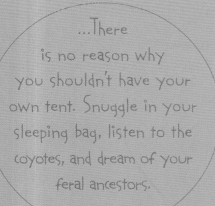

...There is no reason why you shouldn't have your own tent. Snuggle in your sleeping bag, listen to the coyotes, and dream of your feral ancestors.

Finally, let's talk about mountains?

Yes, you have one of those people. Come the weekend it's not the dog park, it's the wilderness park. If you've chosen wisely, you will not be that Yorkie halfway up giant mountain. One shudders at the thought (unless in one of those cunning little packs designed for dogs, much like human babies have—but still, in my opinion, not an ideal way for a delicate flower to spend her day).

You and your person will be quite happy wearing packs filled with food and, well, more food. Breathe the fresh air. Avoid the bears and they will avoid you. Curb yourself—which in the mountains means go off the trail. When you set up camp at night, stare into the campfire and remember how your noble ancestors first taught humans to feed and shelter dogs, around a campfire perhaps not too different from the one before you. And as you snuggle into your person's sleeping bag while the coyotes sing in the distance remember: somewhere up there, Sirius, the dog star is watching over all of us.

chapter four

Your Fashion
Pedigree

avoiding the fashion victim syndrome

Fashion pedigrees are made, not born. It matters not if your father was Ch. Weird Name to the Maximus Degreeus and got shout outs from every dog show judge from here to Crufts. That's just the talk. You, yourself, have to walk the walk right where you live.

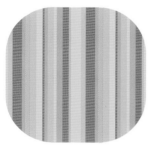

The Elements of Style

First, let's talk fashion faux paws. There are certain things that are just wrong no matter which way the fickle winds of fashion are blowing. Best that you learn the petrosexual's rules now, rather than be slapped across the forehead with the cruel black band of "Fashion Don't."

First, foremost and always: No choke collars (aka training collars) in metal, leather, or nylon except when the collar is at one end of a leash and your person is at the other. Choke collars may sound kinky and cool, but what if it got caught on something? You could literally choke to death, darling. More than one prime pup has met a sad end that way. So don't do it. Besides, except for the taking your person-for-a-walk situation described above, chain collars have all the charm of a biped wearing an ankle bracelet.

...The très petit should pay beaucoup attention to the proportion of clothing.

Argyle is not for the portly. If you're slim and long of limb, wear it with caution, lest you look like a traffic sign.

Lesser (and less dangerous) faux paws include:

faux leather, faux fur, feathers, sequins, anything seasonal. Should you be put into any of these down-market dog items, feel free to bellywalk, roll on your back, hide under the bed or whatever is necessary to convey that this is not your best look.

...Unless you're going to the Oscars, sunglasses and feathers don't mix.

...A little form-fitting shirt brings out the best in a small-figured dog.

Does your person insist on dressing you up for the holidays? The jinglebell collar? The reindeer antlers? Uses your mug on their holiday card?

I once knew a bull terrier who managed to look positively Jack the Ripper while wearing bunny ears. The photograph turned out quite nicely after all, although perhaps it was not what his owner expected. I'm not saying if you can't beat them join them. But if you can't beat them, darling, make it your own. Mine the irony because seasonal frou-frou will never, ever be fashion. But with a little work, at least you can add the attitude that will, one hopes, save you from complete humiliation.

Finally, I must give you a word about theme dressing. It's a bad idea, not only is it tasteless, but it could also be downright dangerous. Think about a dachshund in a hotdog bun outfit. Let's not even go there.

...Infusing your pose with a little attitude will help you through unfortunate photo ops like this.

...When it comes to holiday clothing for animals, there is no such thing as Santa Claus.

Collar vs. Harness

First, leashes will naturally match your collar or harness. That said, I personally think harnesses can make one look quite pudgy if one is not careful. You want, at all times, to maximize your line. On the other hand, if your owner is directionally impaired, it is much easier to guide him or her while wearing a harness. You run less risk of choking yourself when you must, sometimes forcefully, correct your owner's faulty trajectory. Also, a very small dog will find that a harness can add a certain illusion of size. The more leather the better on that little Napoleon. And a harness is so much easier on that dainty little neck.

Do try to prevent your biped from lifting you up by your harness, though. It's so undignified. You're not a piece of luggage, one of those silly, animal-shaped child's purses, or a bowling ball.

...An ill-fitting harness gives one all the dignity of a yoga mat.

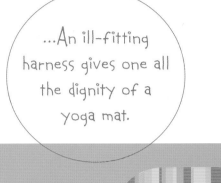

The act of dangling in your harness can also make you look fat—especially to dogs on the ground, some of whom, unfortunately, might think such harness acrobatics make you look fat and tasty.

So here it is: if you are buff and like a harness, or are small and need the extra leather props, go for it. If you can't manage leather, at least insist on a flattering solid color. Otherwise, just say, "collar please."

With collars, discreet designs are sometimes allowed—a nice black and white leather for special occasions, or even a fluorescent orange with reflector stripe if you are going to take your biped for a walk at night. Remember, safety first! Even a collar with a flashing light is permitted after dark. But for everyday, do try to tone it down. You want to wear your collar—you don't want it to wear you. And believe me, a purple fur collar will be all that anyone sees.

...You want to wear your collar—you don't want it to wear you.

And finally, no collars with your name spelled out on it. Please! I mean, do you want to make your name a gift to the whole world? I don't think so.

A couple discreet tags are all you need to accessorize your collar or harness. First and foremost you need one with your person's name and your address and phone number. And of course add your rabies tag and city registration tags where required.

And about those name tags: If your collar or harness is plain, you can make a little personal statement here. You can allow your biped to adorn you with a tag shaped like a bone, or a heart or even- (oh dear) a dog house. But never, ever make it a fire hydrant.

A microchip as additional identification? An excellent idea. It goes with every-thing. And it's so James Bond.

...Is it a collar? Is it a garter? Clothing that can't be readily identified should be strictly avoided.

The Groomed Dog

We city dogs know that sidewalks are mother Nature's nail files. Regular walks not only keep our tummies trim, our constitutions regular, and our spirits serene, but they also file the nails. Still, having your human give your nails a regular once over with nice, sharp, specially designed nail clippers is a good rule of paw. It eliminates potentially nasty and painful splits and chips and prevents that big paw no-no, the curly dewclaw. You do not need a long, curling dewclaw. What are you going to use it for? To snort puppy chow?

An equally big paw no-no is nail polish. Humans do not always use it wisely on their own digits, and they are down right profligate in the use of it on helpless dogs. Okay, a very little dog in a nice doggie carrier or handbag, with a discreet bow and matching nail polish (you Yorkies, Bichons, and Maltese know who you are) is a statement. What kind of statement I leave up to your person, who, it is to be hoped, is not similarly attired.

...Cleanliness is next to dogliness.

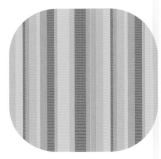

But if your person pants for paw paint, at least prevail upon him or her to keep it subtle. Subtly, it cannot be repeated too often, works for dogs as well as humans. Pale pink, sandy beige, shell, any color that is not passionate putrid painful purple or screaming red will be your best bet. But remember the ultimate rule of paw: no nail polish is good nail polish.

AND FOR

HEAVEN'S SAKE

TRAIN YOUR

PERSON NOT TO

GET SHAMPOO

IN YOUR EYES.

Baths? Well, I am not personally fond of them. I think I smell fine, thank you. And if your person thinks that you need bathing every week (thereby removing valuable protective oils from your coat), then you chose unwisely, at least in this area. Bathing is an occasional requirement in my book—once a month at most, before the regular reapplication of that lovely anti-flea and tick unguent which every dog should demand (except puppies, who are too young to handle the strong stuff).

You never get fleas, darling? Well then, obviously, you poor deprived woof-woof, you never go to the park, or encounter another dog and you certainly never travel. You can get fleas anywhere, and it's better to be prepared. A further shudderworthy note: those little lyme bag ticks have even been found in city parks! So there.

...A good roll in the dirt will remove telltale signs of the dreaded bath.

Human shampoo is not really the best choice, either. The perfumes quite overwhelm the delicate canine nose, and frequently strip our skin and coats of those same oils mentioned above. A nice basic dog shampoo that has emollients to make our coats look their best is the choice of all discriminating dogs. The water should be warm, but not hot, and we should be rinsed thoroughly afterwards. Following the bath ordeal with a vigorous rubdown with a nice big fluffy towel and a good-sized biscuit helps us get over the ordeal. And for heaven's sake. Train your person not to get shampoo in your eyes.

Finally, if you get the chance after a bath, a good roll in something forbidden helps remove that post-bath stress. I always bolt for the bed, myself. Not only does it feel delicious to wriggle away that awful just-had-a-bath feeling, but the screams of my person as she chases me off are, well, just a teensy bit gratifying.

...Un-naturelle.

Hairstyles

Poodles as topiary? What is that about? I'm sure the humans have their reasons (although reason has nothing to do with it, in my humble opinion), but the poodles know they look ridiculous!

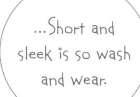

...Short and sleek is so wash and wear.

All dogs need attention paid on a regular basis to their lovely coats. It might be as simple as a regular rub down with a hound mitt, as required for moi, to regular brushing to remove excess hair, as required for huskies, to serious comb outs and once or twice a year removal of undercoats for border terriers and English sheepdogs and so forth.

...Au-naturelle

If you train your person to brush you regularly, you can use this as a bonding experience. Lean against her. Make little noises in your throat. Sigh deeply. Work the awww factor. Not only will this regular attention to follicle fabulousness help you look your best, but it will allow your human to keep an eye on your general outward health in more detail. Early attention to those lumps and bumps (which are generally nothing anyway) can head off trouble and much too much time and money spent at the veterinarian later.

If you are a dog who does need your hair styled, then once again let me strongly suggest you err on the side of simplicity. In fact, two words: puppy cut. Despite the name, it is a charming style for every age, low maintenance and flattering to almost every figure. A nice short puppy do is much preferred over the full body shave I have seen some poor malamutes parading in the park.

Yes, such tonsorial assault makes maintenance easier for the human involved, but that human should be ashamed of himself. Shaving full coated dogs in the summer does them no service. It removes layers that insulate against heat as well as cold, exposes tender skin to sunburn and the dog to peer ridicule.

Puppy cut. Puppy cut. Puppy cut.

The Tailored Dog

Clothing for dogs comes all too close to the fashion faux paws danger zone. A classic Burberry coat is nice for a stroll in the rain, especially if you aren't of the hirsute husky type. But avoid booties except in cases of severe sidewalk salt saturation. So much better to just have your feet wiped off after those messy outings in snow or rain. And cleaner, too.

A note of caution here—plaids, in general, can make one look like a sofa. All that horizontal and vertical activity quickly overwhelms even the most perfect physique, creating the impression of a misshapen TV test pattern. We're meant to sit on ottomans, not be mistaken for them. Besides, if you have the fur for it, do you really need more? You know the answer to that. If, on the other hand, you have short smooth fur, you are going to need a little more protection in cold weather.

Italian greyhounds, for example, almost always need that extra layer except on the warmest days. Fortunately, they have the figures for it. A nice, plain fleece should do the trick. Have your biped shop, or better yet go shopping with her, at the nicer emporiums. Or have your human do a little online credit card exercise. But do curb her enthusiasm for faux leopard, zebra stripes, or cute sayings on sweaters such as: I'm a Little Snow Angel. Do we care?

...Small dogs can pull off so many styles that would make larger-boned breeds look...well...larger.

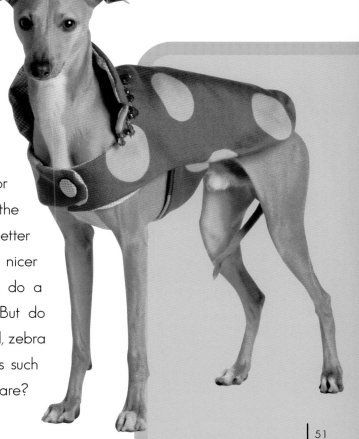

chapter five

Training
Your Human

oh, behave

Training? Didn't we talk about training in the chapter on diet and exercise? No, we did not.

Bark it after me, "A happy human is a well-trained human."

And who's going to train your human to treat you like top dog if not you the consummate petrosexual? A well-trained human can make all the difference in where you sleep, what you eat, exercise routines, and even travel plans.

It begins when you are a puppy. Your human objects to puppy piddle on the floor. Fair enough. You go to the door and bark. Voilà. Your human is soon trained to take you out. This one training tip, if used wisely, can often get you an extra walk. Just make sure not to cry wolf too often.

...Humans are fairly slow-learning creatures so constant practice is essential to their success as house-hold companions.

As you get older, you will find additional training will be useful in promoting a bond between you and your human, even though he is sadly deficient in the language of dogs. But before we dig more deeply into the serious side of human training, let's talk...totally inappropriate human behavior.

Stupid Dog Tricks

You know what they are: playing dead, saying prayers, begging, rolling over. Humiliating, pointless, and demeaning you might even say. Darling, I agree. But consider. This is important to your human. He thinks when he says, "Lulu, play dead," and you go down, he is communicating with you. Why he would want to see what you look like dead—well, let's not go there. And in a sweet, dim way, he is managing to communicate. After all, you understand what he is saying, right? Even if the motivation is a little, well, lost in translation.

He's a good human! So indulge him. Roll over. Give your paw. Beg. But always insist upon a treat, even if you are watching your figure. The key to training a human (apart from patience, patience, patience) is consistency. Don't let him think for one single trick that you are going down this road for free.

Commands every human should learn:

- *Sit*
- *Stay*
- *Come*
- *Down*
- *Heel*

Once you have established a reasonable rate of trick and treat exchange, you can move on.

Real Human Tricks

No, I don't mean having your human roll over, beg and play dead. Although it would be fun, wouldn't it? I mean sit, stay, down, and come. And, oh yes, heel. All basic, easy commands to teach your human, if you do it right.

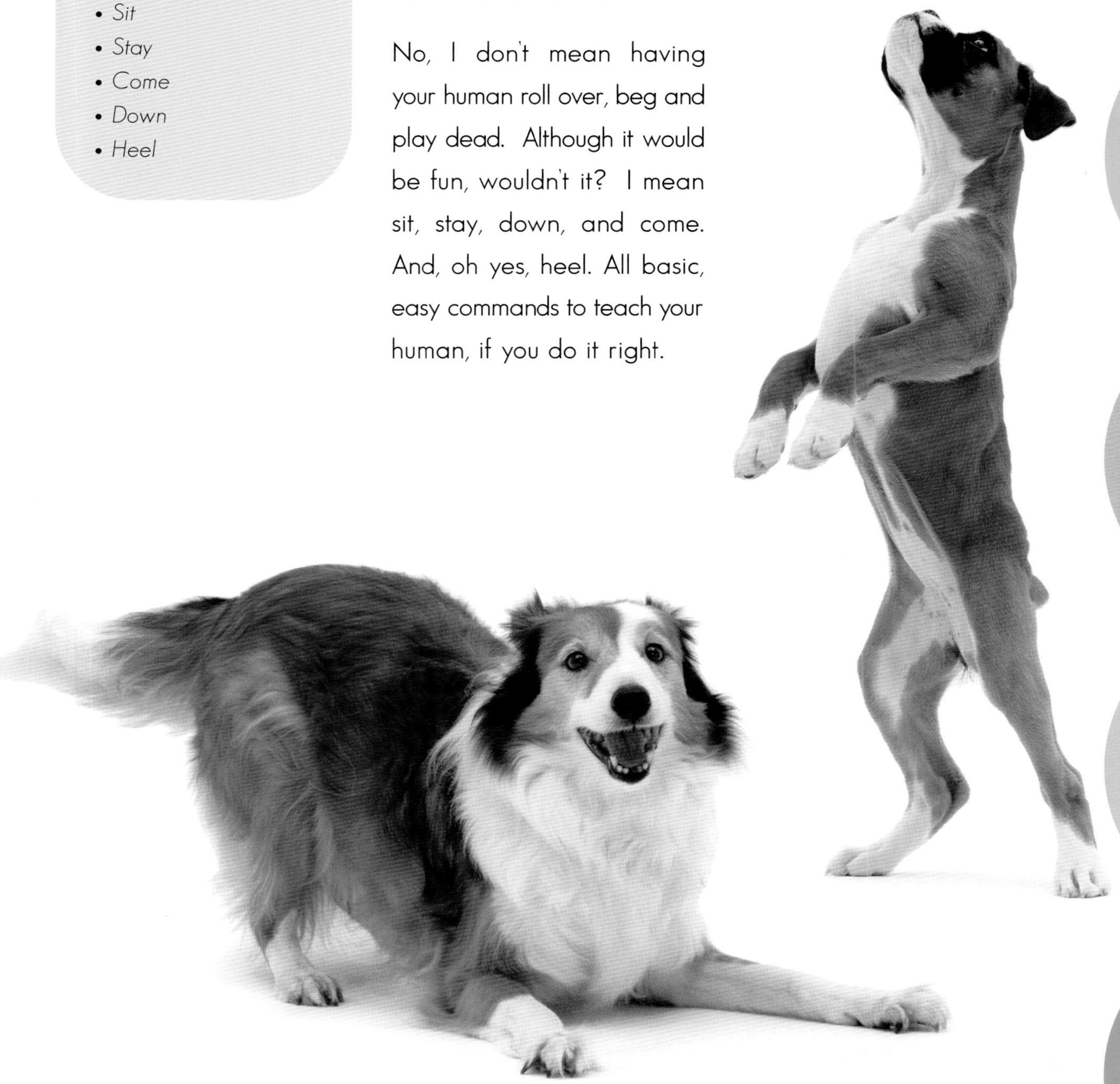

Sit. Agreeing with your human on when to sit couldn't be more important. When your human says sit, and you sit, it makes you look good to your human and it makes your human look good to the other humans.

And make no mistake—although human pack order is less overtly about what you sniff and mark and when, it still depends a great deal on who seems able to boss whom around. Thus, in the human mind, two humans meeting one another, each accompanied by a dog, are two pack leaders at summit. The least you can do in that situation is make your human look good by choosing to sit when asked..

Stay. Well, of course. Why not? There's somewhere you had to be, maybe? Stay like a good dog (except, of course, in case of fire, out of control car or grandma in the well). Work with your human until you both get it right. Encourage him to use hand signals as well as his voice for all commands. That way, even in noisy situations, you'll always be able to communicate.

Come. Why should you have to come when you're called? Do cats? No. Well, you're not a cat, are you, and thank Sirius for that. Picture this: You're out for a stroll in the park. This park, which understands dogs, allows them to be off leash before 9:00 a.m. And your owner trusts you not to run away. Why? Because you've trained him to use the "come" command.

...Human-canine partnerships must give the human the illusion that the human is in charge.

Nevertheless, because it is a beautiful day in the neighborhood, you wander absent-mindedly away (you beagles know who you are).

You smell the flowers then olafactor the garbage. You exchange a few friendly insults with the nearest acorn-brain in a squirrel suit. All of a sudden you look up only to discover that your person isn't where you left him. He is lost! For a panic-stricken moment, you consider running through the park, howling his name. Then you remember the dog catchers. Best not to draw attention to yourself—yet.

You begin to retrace your steps, trying to remember if you've been micro-chipped, and if so where. You pause. Here is where you smelled the flower. There is where you caught the divine scent of a ripening pastrami sandwich. Pastrami...for a moment you are able to shut out the horrible images from that show on Animal Planet about what happens to lost pets.

Then you hear his voice calling, "Gracie! Come!" Well, aren't you just the happiest dog that you've trained your person so well? This is the reward for all that hard work. You are able to trot merrily up to your biped, who is now clutching the cup of coffee he wandered so carelessly away to purchase. For a moment, you consider jumping up on him in your joy, until you remember the coffee. You wag your tail and smile.

"Good human," you say. "Good dog," he says.

And best of all, he thinks you are so smart for doing what he asks.

Down. Not as much fun. Why would your person want you to put your belly on a dirty city sidewalk? On the other hand, down is perfectly acceptable while visiting other bipeds in their homes. Sitting allows you to keep an eye on things in such scenarios, but can be tiring. But if you are in a down, stay situation, you can catch a little beauty rest.

So, yes, down has its uses (not to be confused with your human saying, "Off, off get off," usually shrieked if you've gone muddy paws first up onto the bed your human shares with you, or, "Naughty dog," after you have jumped up inappropriately. But more about that later.

Heel. Heel simply means walking nicely on your person's left side, close to her left heel. Purists will want their dogs to have their noses more or less even with their left leg (the biped leg, that is) and be mere inches from said leg.

...When you're cute, it's especially important to be firm with your human.

But for most purposes outside a show ring, a somewhat looser interpretation of the heel command is permitted. And frankly, on very crowded city sidewalks, where pausing to scratch and sniff is unworkable, trotting along at your biped's heel, letting her do all the work of pushing through the teeming masses and not having to worry about some clumsy, possibly dog-unfriendly human falling over you, is quite nice.

WHEN YOU HAVE

WORKED LONG

ENOUGH WITH

YOUR OWNER, YOU

WILL FIND THAT

YOU AGREE ON

MANY THINGS.

...You can teach an old human new tricks.

When you have worked long enough with your owner, either by encouraging him to go over one of the excellent dog books or training videos out there or (much more fun) by joining a training class, you will find that you agree on many things such as when it is okay to jump up enthusiastically (playing romp in the leaf games) and when it is a big barking NO (like when she's wearing her suit for work and as previously mentioned, holding a cup of coffee). You will agree to lie down and stay and in return, your person will take you to visit other people. Those other people can be encouraged to give you treats not only for the stupid dog tricks but also for the most basic commands.

If you work very hard with your person, you might convince him to get a therapy dog certification, and then you can take him to visit hospitals or nursing homes. Yes, I mean it. Before you say, "Gag me with a chicken bone, I hate the veterinarian's and I'm not going to any stinking hospital," remember that a well-rounded dog does his share of volunteer work, and in turn sets a good example for his human. As a volunteer visitor to hospitals, schools, or senior residences or care centers, you are an ambassador for all dogs. Better yet, you are the center of all attention. You get lots of praise and pats—and even more treats. In addition, if you are a certified therapy dog, certain airlines will allow you to fly where all good dogs should fly—with your human in the cabin.

So consider volunteer work for your biped (even if it does require you to wear stupid pet outfits during certain holidays). But most importantly, start her training early no matter what her age or temperament when you get her. And don't give up. You *can* teach an old human new tricks.

City Dog
Country Dog

happiness is always knowing where your tail is

As you stroll through the streets of your fair city, you will notice many dogs walking their owners. But not all of the sidewalk society are the same. Some are, how do you say it? Oh, yes—rude.

An off-leash dog racing down a city sidewalk is not a pretty sight. The mere thought of it makes me curl my upper lip, in spite of myself, in a most unattractive way.

As a dog (well, technically, bitch) who prefers to be introduced to other dogs properly, I abhor the lunging lout who scrambles up to me and dives into my face nose first. Even more do I resent being sternly told to, "Stop It!" when I express my displeasure at this rude dog's behavior! OUT-rageous!

...Some dogs have no sense of boundaries.

...Without manners, dogs are just...well... people.

It is not my fault this creature has failed to train her owner on when and how to use a leash, not my fault that she lacks common sidewalk courtesy, not my fault she behaves like a rube who just out fell out of the back of the pick-up truck (where, frankly, she shouldn't have been riding in the first place). So what if her owner is trailing behind, bleating, "She's friendly. Muff-muff loves everybody." But does everybody love Muff-muff? Decidedly not.

...Who loves her?

...Excellent question!

You itch to teach the upstart a lesson. But you cannot. Your owner has already told you to stop it. Now he undoubtedly will tell you to sit. And stay. You sit. You stay. You raise the fur on the ruff of your neck and bare a sliver of tooth hoping your person will not notice.

Of course, in petrosexual language, that is shouting, and it is to be hoped that Muff-muff gets it. Because if she doesn't, one day sooner or later, she is going to meet a less polite dog with a less well-trained owner. And then she is going to get It good. Poor Muff-muff. Can you really blame her? If dog and human do not work together to enforce the rules of polite behavior, then who will?

Speaking of polite behavior, let us talk pre-sidewalk manners.

Exiting the Building

If you live in a building without an elevator, you do not pull your owner down the stairs in the mad rush to get outside. A dead owner, having fallen down three flights, cannot take you for walks. Ever again.

As you make your happy way down the stairs, you may, of course express your joy by wagging your tail and, if you must, a little enthusiastic tongue-lolling. While on the stairs, stay next to the railing. Give others room to pass.

...There is a right and wrong way to exit a building.

Should you be fortunate enough to live in an elevator building (I love a good five floor walk-up, myself, but it can be difficult, especially as one gets older), remember that the same basic rules apply: Sit. Stay. Do not jump up. Sit next to the elevator wall to give others space—and to prevent having your tail trod upon. In fact, city dog rule number one: Happiness in the city is always knowing where your tail is.

HAPPINESS IN THE

CITY IS ALWAYS

KNOWING WHERE

YOUR TAIL IS.

If you are allowed on subways or buses (and well-trained dogs, especially those with special dog passes should be, at least in certain designated sections of the bus or subway) then that is the way to go. I mean, if the bipeds want fewer cars in the city and less pollution, don't force dog owners to drive to the park. Good grief!

Now, where was I? Oh yes—continue to sit, stay and watch your tail, in a nice, tight heel close to your person. If all dogs behaved in this way, we would soon see ourselves not just beside the bus but in it.

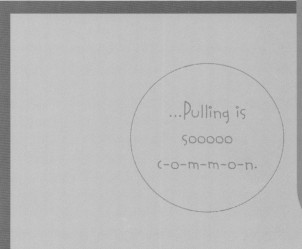

...A lady never pulls

...Pulling is sooooo c-o-m-m-o-n.

Personal Hygiene

As you know, the term "walking the dog" often, if not always, is a human way of saying that you are going out to pee and poop. The well-equipped owner of course carries pooper scooper bags (the home delivery bags of the large metropolitan newspapers, particularly that nice blue *New York Times* one, are excellent, and you're recycling, you canine good citizen) or nice thick pieces of newspaper for the total decomposable package. The well-trained owner can read the signals and know when you are ready to allow him to put his pooper scooper bag to good use. Together you veer toward the curb. Voilà. The deed is done. You watch proudly as your owner turns the bag inside out over his hand, reaches down, scoops the poop, turns the bag right side out, ties it off at the top, and deposits your deposit in the nearest trash can.

...Les accoutrements de toilettes .

Together, you are doing your bit to keep your city clean and setting an example (wasted, no doubt, but one must always try) for those cretinous bipeds who do not clean up after their less fortunate dogs. As for territorial marking, do try to avoid the cunningly planted flowerbeds surrounding the trees outside the apartment buildings.

It is a cliché, but it is true—fire hydrants and meters make excellent calling card scent holders. I also like to mark the wheels of the truly large and stupid-looking SUVs hogging all the parking space on my blocks.

Now, having mastered the city dog basics, let's move on.

The Dog Run

As mentioned before, you adhere to the rules of etiquette at the dog run. But some modifications apply. Since you are all off-leash, more exuberant approaches to one another are allowed. After all, you wouldn't be there if you didn't want to sniff and greet, would you? Share your toys. If you are not of a sharing nature and are going to go all toothy and pack leader over a mere tennis ball, then don't allow your owner to bring one for you. Dogs who fight in dog runs are not invited back. And fighting is tacky, especially when there are so many other ways to settle differences.

While in the run, you may dig, but do not crater the place. Confine your pee and poop moments to edges of the run. Make sure your owner picks up after you. Be sure, as you run and play, to pause to check in with your owner from time to time. It makes him feel good and it makes you look good. And don't overdress. It's a play-group, darling, not the bow wow ball. Wear a plain collar or harness that can stand up to rough and tumble.

Sidewalks, In Conclusion

Concerning life in the city, let me just say the following:

You may hate motorcycles, but you do not hurl insults at them as they pass. They cannot hear you. Trust me. You must walk on by the insolent deli cat who sticks her tail straight up at you. You may not speak cat, but you can read sign language. Nevertheless, you ignore the insult.

And delicious as the garbage of summer is, spilling out from the cans, you do not eat it. You will not like going outside at 3:00 a.m. because what goes in must come out —now. Neither will your person.

Nor will you ever permit your person to tie you up outside to some parking meter or tree where any dog snatcher might make away with you and either keep you against your will or, hellishly worse, better you should die right then, sell you to a research facility. It happens. So don't let your human put you in that deadly peril.

As a complete city dog, you know how to handle these mean streets. And sidewalks.

You are the dog. The city stinks. It's simply bitchin'. Isn't it heavenly? Enjoy it to its ripest. But obey the rules.

...Well-bred dogs don't eat garbage.

THAT LOVELY, RIPE, AROMATIC GARBAGE MAY LOOK DELICIOUS BUT THINK TWICE BEFORE EATING IT. YOU'LL MORE THAN LIKELY END UP TAKING AN UNSCHEDULED TRIP WITH A POOPER SCOOPER.

Rules for City Life

- Thou shalt refrain from reacting to the provocations of ill-trained humans and their companion dogs

- Thou shalt not drag thy human helter-skelter down the stairs

- Thou shalt know where thy tail is at all times

- Thou shalt make sure thy human picks up after thee

- Thou shalt share thy toys at the dog run or thou shalt not bring them

- Thou shalt not bark at motorcycles

- Thou shalt not eat out of garbage cans, lest thou have to make a late night trip to the sidewalk

- Thou shalt ignore the insults of the fiendish feline at all costs, as those costs will be high

...Dogs who know the rules, rule.

The Country

Ah, but in the country, it is a different world! In the country no one knows who you are. You can dig holes in flowerbeds, romp madly through the fields, and chase the neighbor's cat or even those delightful chickens. You are a free dog. A wild dog. *A dog in trouble.* Unleashing your inner dog on your neighbor's tulip bed is the surest road to perdition.

As to that little house in the Hamptons or the cottage deep in New Hampshire or a villa in Napa, the rules for inside behavior still apply. But when you're outside fling off that leather collar for something a little more lightweight or night visible. Make sure the tags are firmly attached though! Take a howl or two at the moon if you must. But remember moderation in all things.

UNLEASHING YOUR INNER DOG ON YOUR NEIGHBOR'S TULIP BED IS THE SUREST ROAD TO PERDITION

...With a coat like this, who needs clothes?

...Sunglasses are a must in the country

You must still ignore the neighbor's cat, interesting though it is when she offers you that exact same insult as the deli fiend. Yes, cat insults are universal. And your response must be a universal, "I couldn't be more bored."

If your human is addicted to hosting large gatherings for social interaction (even though he or she or they might have come to the country to "get away from it all") interact politely with Yippy and Peppy and any other dogs that come with the human houseguests. Stand quietly as they approach you, wagging your tail slightly. As you know, this more or less upright tail wag means, "I don't know if you are friend or foe, so I am withholding judgment." If Yippy and Peppy have not trained their owners as well as you have trained yours, do not think just because they jump up on sofas and humans and steal food and beg inappropriately that you can do the same. Remember, you live here. They, on the other hand, may well not be invited back. If they are not up to your standards, remain calm and aloof. With any luck, you'll never have to deal with them again.

With regard to neighboring dogs, do let the dog who lives in the nearby house approach you first. If he wants to be friendly, accept the friendship. Remember, you are not in the city now, and any help you can get in navigating the local territory and rules will be useful. Do not talk too much of your city life. It will sound like boasting. Do not wander off (even if your person leaves you outside) unprotected by a fence or you may quickly find that you really are lost. Again, beagles and other scent hounds, take particular note.

And the very unmannerly animals you meet will not be helpful if you go astray. The small black-and-white striped ones, for example, have truly awesome spraying capacity, worthy of a small fire truck. They are called skunks. Avoid them! If you meet one, do not engage. Turn and run. They may look small and harmless and as if they might be fun to bark at, but if they decide to mark you (a bad habit among skunks in general), you are going to smell really bad. And not in a good way.

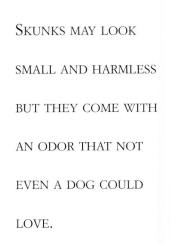

SKUNKS MAY LOOK SMALL AND HARMLESS BUT THEY COME WITH AN ODOR THAT NOT EVEN A DOG COULD LOVE.

Your friends, both city dogs and country dogs, will laugh at you. You will be subject to exile from the human habitation. You might possibly be sent to the veterinarian. Many baths will be involved, none of them involving the nicer dog shampoos. Some may even involve tomato juice, which humans believe offsets the dreadful smell. Can you say ick?

The animals that look prickly are prickly. They're called porcupines. And they are more than willing to share their quills in up close dog and porcupine encounters. And when you slap yourself upside the head with a porcupine, it hurts.

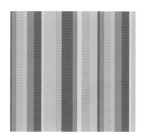

Those quills are barbed and they go in deep, and they are equipped to stay deep. Pawing, rolling, and rubbing your face just make it worse. If you had your mouth open, you're going to have a mouthful of big, fat quills. Unless, of course, you tackled a very young porcupine, then they're going to look like needles and feel just as unpleasant.

Some bipeds use pliers to pull out the quills, but you will find it best to make a little trip to, yes, the veterinarian, where if you are lucky, you'll get a nice dose of anaesthesia before the quill removal process begins. Afterwards, you will be groggy, possibly sick to your stomach, probably required to take antibiotics, and sore. Can you say ouch?

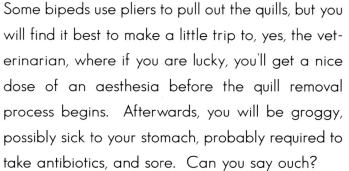

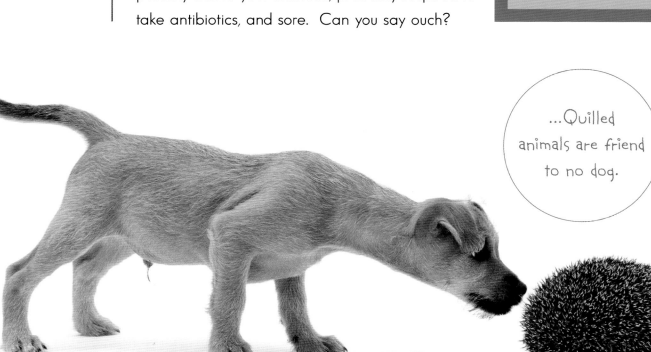

...Quilled animals are friend to no dog.

If you are in bear country, be prepared. Bears do not like the smell of dogs, in general, and since dogs have been used to hunt bears, who can blame them? Don't take it personally, and don't try to reason with the bear. If you encounter a bear on a trail or in the woods, leave. Do it quietly and quickly, and hope you do it before the bear sees you and makes up its mind to pursue you. Just remember, in a bear-dog encounter, the bear wins. Think of them as the automobiles of the woods. Don't chase them and don't get caught under their wheels.

The large brown quadrupeds often equipped with antlers, are uniformly brown, and found in woods and fields are deer. Don't chase them. You can't catch them; you could easily get lost while in pursuit; and hunters like to think that they are the only ones entitled to chase and kill deer. If it's hunting season and a hunter sees you chasing a deer, that hunter may decide to take a shot at you.

...In dog-bear encounters, the smaller animal never wins.

Which brings me to hunting season.

In hunting season, stay out of the woods. Requiring your person to wear bright orange or day-glow pink and putting enough bells on both of you to make you look like candidates for Santa's sled beasts (a fashion statement so appallingly hideous I marvel that it doesn't put people off hunting just by its sheer vulgarity) is all very well, and if you walk in the middle of the day on well-travelled human trails, you are probably safe. But remember that they are armed and you are not.

...It's naughty to chase sheep.

Is it worth risking your life to tiptoe through the leaves during hunting season? No. Bad enough that the deer and the rest of the animals have to put up with it, but you can avoid it. So do. Make your human find out when and where men (mostly) will be tricking themselves out in camouflage and hunter's plaid and bright orange, and toting their big guns into the woods, and don't go there. Literally. And when it is not hunting season, well, just stick to the trails, more or less. That way you'll be sure to live to thank me for all my excellent advice. Meanwhile, those other more or less horned beasts in the fields are cows. Cows belong to farmers, and farmers will, in some instances, shoot you on sight for messing with their bovine possessions. The same holds true for creatures covered with white wool, also known as sheep. You sleep, perhaps, on a sheepskin, either faux or real, but you do not chase sheep. Once again, Farmer Brown is almost certainly equipped with a rifle, and may not be averse to using it.

CHASING DEER

IS POINTLESS

UNLESS YOU ARE

A DEERHOUND

In fact, all the animals near barns, whether in pens or out, should be avoided. Pigs smell good, but inch for inch they outweigh you and out-mean you, trust me. Chickens, ducks and geese can set up a satisfying cacophony when chased, but thou shalt not. Unless you are a working sheep or cattle dog invited to work, leave the farm animals alone. Don't try to be a country dog when you are not. You are a summer dog, a weekender. Learn the local rules and abide by them. You'll be glad you did.

Rules for Country Life

- *Thou shalt not chase thy neighbor's cat*

- *Thou shalt run with abandon, though only in designated areas*

- *Thou shalt be tolerant of visiting houseguests and their people despite their lack of proper training*

- *Thou shalt avoid encounters with skunks and porcupines lest thou suffer extreme physical discomfort*

- *Thou shalt not seek out bear, for any direction in which a bear is heading is the wrong direction for thee*

- *Thou shalt not chase farm animals unless thou has been bred or employed to do so*

chapter seven

Cats and Insignificant Others

do you really want to be the leader of the pack?

Well, yes. You want to be leader of the pack. But no matter what, it has to happen sooner or later. Things change. You've got a perfect pack. The humans think they're large and in charge. Training is going beautifully. You just use your doghouse for laughs. If it is just you and your human, well, let's talk.

Significant Others

Humans, in general, mate. It is a fact of life. And the criteria they use to choose a mate is, often, if not always, puzzling. But that is not your problem. Your problem is if the proposed biped mate is dog-worthy. If it is a casual date—those events which are the human equivalent to a good base-of-tail sniff and dog park romp—then remain friendly but aloof, unbending (but not unyielding of course) for treats.

You can even perform a few tricks, if you are so inclined. Or you might prefer to stake your claim to your human when the possibly unsuitable mate says, "Play dead" by giving the presumptuous biped a puzzled yet reproving look that says, "Over my dead body or possibly yours."

...Over my dead body...or possibly yours.

If things progress beyond the play date, monitor the dining situation. Your human may be dining out much more in this stage of the mating ritual. If they are going for the tiny, expensive meals at the exclusive restaurants then you are forewarned and out of luck. However, if they continue to dine at places with generous portions (however unfamiliar the cuisine) where they can bring home doggie bags, this is good.

The new person should be either familiar with dog requirements or willing to be trained in that particular point of etiquette. If they have moved beyond the dog park and the restaurant reservations, we come to the next important point: Are they willing to let you sleep on the bed? This is tricky because you may not want to invoke the right of parley in the initial stages of bed sharing arrangements. If you insist on your rightful spot you may find yourself in for a bumpy ride. Human mating rituals, not to put too fine a point on it, frequently involve the loss of sheets, pillows, and inhibitions in ways unimaginable in dog mating rituals.

IF YOUR HUMAN BECOMES INVOLVED WITH A SIGNIFICANT OTHER, YOU MIGHT WISH TO RETREAT TO YOUR OWN SPACE OR CLAIM A FORMERLY OFF-LIMITS PIECE OF FURNITURE

So do a judicious and discreet survey of the situation. If it looks like it's going to be a long night, or a lot of long nights, claim a chair—perhaps the one you've always wanted but never been allowed on—settle in. Now's the time to make your move.

...Dogs make much better sleeping partners than humans.

Trust me. This stage will pass and the object d'amour will either move on or move in. The benefits of your biped having a significant other include doggie bags and the possibility of claiming formerly prohibited furniture.

At the moving in point, things should have settled down. You can then, if you so desire, reestablish your bed rights (while being careful not to relinquish any new furniture territory you may have acquired—it doesn't hurt to be prepared). If your human has chosen wisely, this should not be difficult. If the other has acquired significance (and at the moving-in stage one must assume that they have) it is up to you to assist your human in training the new pack member.

For example, do they understand W-A-L-K? Because face it, taking an elegant pair of humans to the park for a walk is fun—especially if they both play ball. (They do like to play ball, don't they?)

...When should you invoke the right of parley?

If not, what is your human thinking? Be firm. Be patient. Just as in the initial stages of training your primary biped, you must be consistent. The rules might be changing, but it doesn't mean all of them have to change. A second human can be a big benefit, if you manage it wisely. It is, in large part, up to you.

Other Animals

Yes, it's true. Cats. And Dogs. The significant other may come with an animal of his or her own. In fact, that may be how the two bipeds met. And if they did meet over you and the other dog, then good work! Less good if the other was carrying a cat in the veterinarian's waiting room, as once happened to a good friend of mine. There she was, sick as a, well, dog, and her person starts chatting up a guy with a cat carrier. The addition of other animals into the household can create stress. It is up to you to set and define the terms.

...Tail height and speed of wag are key to setting the proper note of non-threatening authority when a cat comes into your home.

But really the truth about other cats and dogs is that they're not so bad—as long as you are the top dog. As they enter your kingdom, hoist your tail to medium, wag very slowly, and greet them kindly, if not enthusiastically. Make it clear that you are master of your domain. Do not allow the creature to insinuate herself too quickly. After an appropriate amount of time has passed and (I cannot stress this strongly enough) when your biped is in the room, allow the new animal to curl up with you, if it so desires. Failing that, curl up near it and give your human a long, understanding look from the big browns.

The awww factor is great. Your person will call the other person in to see the good dog (you). It will be worth it. And you may find that, after all, you've gained a most acceptable new member of your pack. Even if it is a cat.

But there is more. Now we must talk of other matters.

...Awww

Steps to Incorporate a New Cat into Your Pack

- *Raise tail to a medium height*
- *Adjust tail speed to a slow wag*
- *Maintain a slight sense of aloofness*
- *With your biped in the room, allow cat to curl up next to you*

Babies

Oh, please. I'm not going to talk about how they're made. Didn't you pay attention in the section on where to sleep? Babies, let us say, happen. And when they do, they change everything. Your biped and his mate. The other cat or dog. But before you crawl into bed and pull the covers over your head, try to get some perspective on babies. Appalling, aren't they? Let's try again. It helps to think of them as biped puppies. They are helpless and have to be guarded, fed, and house trained. And it takes much longer for humans to grow up. There will be years of food falling from table to floor (where you'll be waiting); years of toys (which you'll help the baby to share); years of walks and play dates in the park (in which you'll naturally participate). In fact, since this baby is your human's baby, it is yours too.

So let's talk about NANA. You remember Nana (the nursemaid dog in *Peter Pan*)? Nursemaid—so not you, right? Frumpy outfits, Mary Poppins parapluie. You didn't want puppies, much less a baby. But you've got one and there is no turning back. Remember that your humans, at this point, are undoubtedly in shock and possibly questioning the wisdom of the whole baby decision themselves. If you get into Nana mode for them, you'll have a chance to make yourself an invaluable member of the pack, and you'll rack up big points for style all over town—no matter what Mary Poppins wore. The petrosexual does this with becoming grace.

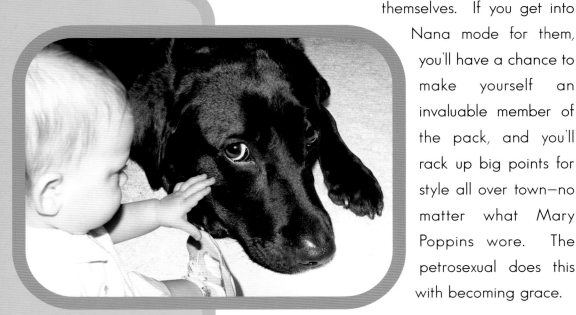

...Babies are simply human puppies.

Be gently enthusiastic about the human puppy. It does smell good, doesn't it, especially when its nappies have been compromised? If the parents are well-trained, they will not leave the baby alone with you so you will not have your tail pulled or your eyes poked. In time, the baby will be housebroken and trained. And if you wait long enough, and are patient enough, the baby will grow up to be a biped also useful for walks, playing ball, and dishing out treats. You may even one day find yourself strolling along with the now maturing child and realize you quite like it, are in fact proud of the job you have done, with the help of your bipeds. Should your bipeds have yet another puppy, er, baby, and find themselves devoting all their time to it, by all means, do the Nana bit. But remember, the baby you raised might possibly feel neglected and left out. He will need you more than ever. And you'll know what to do. Good dog. Good baby.

...Canines can be the first point of civilized contact for the new baby.

The Benefits of Having a Biped Baby in the House

- *If properly trained you will eventually be able to take them for walks, play ball with them, and get snacks from them*

- *Their compromised nappies smell heavenly*

- *They let food fall from their plates*

- *They will laugh at your charming antics*

chapter eight

Veterinarians

do go there

You were just a little thing when it happened, weren't you? But you remember it. And how much fun it was—not! There you were, a helpless puppy standing on a cold metal table being pinched and prodded. You had thermometers poked in one end and fingers poked in the other and needles stuck into you in between. Furthermore, this was being done to you in a room that can only be described as baby-poo yellow. Even as a color-blind puppy you knew that, and it offended your delicate sensibilities even more.

Fast-forward to now. You're a big dog. But not much has changed. Okay, let's face it—the veterinarian's office lacks style. A hanging plant, a few framed certificates, maybe an industrial-style clock, some dog-eared magazines, a floor designed to hide dirt are all that's there for decor. And the smell—it's enough to make a dog puke. No surprise that so many do.

I mean, what do they use to mop the floors with: eau de disgusting? But we're not here to give veterinarians an extreme (because that's what it would take) makeover. After all, sometimes an office is just an office. You're here because you've trained your human to bring you in for regular checkups. It's what any responsible dog does. And it's not the style of the place but what goes on behind those doors that counts.

Is the place clean (apart from the disgusting disinfectant smell that must only bother dogs)? Because cleanliness is next to dogliness. Is the staff nice, friendly, patient, and understanding? In short, the human ideal of the ideal dog? Do they wear cute scrubs? Ones that, presumably, do not match the baby-puke yellow walls? Are there treats in jars on the counter? Do they share their treats in a timely and generous fashion?

Do they keep you waiting while a parade of insufferable cats passes before you? No?

Good. Then when it is your turn, follow your person through the doors into the waiting room with a minimum of resistance. You may whine, just a little, to let your biped know that you are anxious but brave. But then, be brave.

Even if the cubicle, as personal space, lacks everything, the stainless steel table looms, and your human gets the only chair, you must be noble. Remember, your human is no doubt nervous, too. If you focus on her, and on reassuring her, you will find it is not so bad.

Encourage your human to read the brochures with words like "heartworm" and "vaccination program" on them that have taken the place of the dog-eared magazines in the waiting room. This information might well be useful in keeping up your standard of health and living.

At last, the doctor comes in. She's been well trained, too. She approaches you calmly and pets you to say hello, scratching that favorite spot of yours behind your ears. As always, you are impressed. But then, by the smell of her, she has dogs, too. She and your human make a fuss over what they call vaccinations, but really, you hardly notice. Still, accept the praise for being a good dog and a brave dog. But don't hang around. As soon as you can, jump off that cold table. And you might here make a wee exception and give your person a gentle tug toward the door.

And then it is over. The new rabies tag looks just like the old one. A bore. While your human pays the bill, you accept a few more dog biscuits from the expertly prepared staff. And you are particularly pleased knowing that you have set a good example for your human.

Because if you, the petro-sexual, don't, darling, who will?

...Despite the obvious temptation, biting the vet is extremely poor etiquette.

...Elizabethan collars went out with, well, Elizabeth I. And it doesn't make them seem modern to call them E-collars.

Enduring That Trip to the Vet

- Ignore the baby-poo-yellow walls

- Whine slightly to show that you're brave but anxious

- Try not to be too judgmental of the decor (or lack thereof)

- Expect treats in a timely and generous fashion

The Well-Traveled Dog

day care is a dog's best friend

Dogs whose humans work or travel have always faced the challenge of being alone at some point. In the past, the options for dog care were limited: being sent to a kennel or being left in the care of a companion of one's human. But there are now other more interesting options for the modern petrosexual.

My first recommendation is a dog walker. These angels in human form are a must for the dog who has a working human. You absolutely must insist on someone coming in at least once a day to relieve you of the need to nap and chew and wait for your person to come home (and to allow you, frankly, to relieve yourself). A reputable dog walker with good credentials and plenty of dog and street smarts will fill the bill nicely.

But if your human must work for a living, then I have another option for you: doggie daycare.

No longer do you have to endure the kennel where you run to one end, bark, then run to the other end, bark. In the past, the only other alternative would have been using your teeth as weapons of mass destruction, mowing down table and chair leg and anything else in your path. Of course this is socially unacceptable. But if you have trained your human properly, you should not have to resort to such drastic measures. At doggie day care, you get dropped off in the morning, picked up at the end of the working day. In between, it is, literally, if you so desire, all fun and games.

...Look for a daycare facility that has separate running areas for large dogs and small dogs. After all, do you really think Chihuahuas can keep up with greyhounds?

At the daycare facility you will find pleasures of every kind from physical to intellectual. There is really something for every dog. Playful dogs will love the large rooms full of interesting toys. Social dogs will enjoy the company of lots of other dogs, at least some of whom are bound to share your interests or at least be good for a little shop talk.

All dogs will salivate over treats!

Who wouldn't enjoy the people and dogs coming and going. Beds upon which to lounge and possibly even your own television tuned to, naturally, Animal Planet, or even a DVD player showing my all time personal favorite, *Homeward Bound.* (Although the American bulldog should have been played by a bull terrier, as in the original book, *The Incredible Journey,* but we'll let that pass).

Ten Movies Every Dog Should See at Least Once

- *101 Dalmatians*
- *Beethoven*
- *Benji*
- *Best in Show*
- *The Adventures of Milo and Otis*

- *The Incredible Journey*
- *Lady and the Tramp*
- *My Dog Skip*
- *Old Yeller*
- *White Fang*

...Appreciation of culture is a natural part of the Petrosexual's development.

For the dog who is fortunate enough to travel, day care centers often have options for extended stays. But my recommendation if you travel is to hold out for a really upscale doggie B&B. Check it out: Your own room with your own bed; a television; a turndown every night, with a doggie treat upon the pillow. These facilities are on the par with human spas.

But do you really need the homemade doggie treats in the afternoon, too?

Absolutely. And you'd like to sign up for the dog massage, please. Pet me! All over! Don't stop!

...You call it petting. I call it massage.

Okay, it's a little over the top. You'd never let your human get away with some of these well, frankly, extreme spaces. But sometimes, too much of a good thing is a good thing. Enjoy it. It's just a vacation. It's not real life.

You'd like to see a little more of the world, you say, then just the park and the country house?

Daycare is nice, but don't you feel fenced in?

There are many ways for the modern petro-sexual to travel. How about a road trip, you say? Car travel is one of the best ways for dogs of any size to travel.

...Buckle up. It's the law...well maybe it's not the law...but it should be.

I don't care if it's Mr. Rust Bucket, a fully loaded Beamer, a big yawn SUV or even one of those even bigger yawn suburban assault vehicles. You must have your own space in the vehicle, darling. Insist on it. If you've claimed part of the back seat, you need your own plush blanket. You'll need a dog seat belt, too. I know, it's bound to clash with what you're wearing, but it's only for the car. And I have seen the harness attachments in basic black. Do your homework and you can be safety prepared without being fashion impaired. But even with an ugly but serviceable seat belt, better a little clash than a fatal crash, no? Anyway, with luck you've got your own crib in the very back of the car, complete with bed, bones, and toys.

Now sit. Stare out the window. Bark when you see cows. That gives your person a chance to say, "They're only cows, silly." Learn the signs of all the fast food joints. Who told you real dogs don't eat at McDonald's? It's the dog food of the gods—hold the pickle.

...Someday, dogs will be allowed to drive. It can't be that difficult...people do it.

At the same time, don't be afraid to sample the local specialties when on the road. A truly cosmopolitan dog can handle anything. Dungeness crab? Bring it on. Pit barbecue? Go whole hog. Use your nose to expand your human's horizons—except for broccoli. Just say no to broccoli. Gas, darling. It's the last thing you want to share in the car.

...Given our flexible dispositions and appreciation for gustatory diversity, dogs are natural travelers.

Make frequent stops to smell the scenery. And don't forget to remind your person not to leave you in the car if the day is even a little bit warm. Even with the windows down. It just doesn't do. How shall I put this tactfully? Can you say oven? That's what a car is after less than ten minutes in the sun on a moderately warm day. Any car. Price is no object. And dogs left in those cars can die. Not my preferred method of exit, thank you very much. It just doesn't make for a pretty memory picture, if you know what I mean. Do you want your human to remember you that way? And feel guilty?

Whew! I'm glad I got that off my chest.

Flying? Oooh, France, I hope. The French are so civilized about dogs. But wherever you travel, get papered. Dog is in the details. You know, the shot records, the registrations, and all the little details. Make sure the country of your destination will let you in. (Unlike England! Not to mention that our own Hawaii will not. Shame on you!) Then make sure you have the right shots and papers.

I once knew a dog who was planning a lovely trip abroad. But upon arrival, she discovered she was lacking certain crucial papers. She spent a perfectly hellish weekend while it was being sorted out in some terrible little kennel in the middle of nowhere—without television, eating down-market kibble!

...Finally, someone has thought to design canine transport devises that have sophistication and style as opposed to resembling a box of laundry detergent.

BEFORE YOU TRAVEL,

PLAN, PLAN, AND

PLAN. MAKE A LIST.

CHECK IT TWICE.

So, before you travel, plan, plan, and plan. Make a list and check it twice. Arrange to have your own little travel bag complete with all your accoutrements: favorite toys, special meds, extra collar, tags and leads, and those papers, plus a list of everything inside the bag. In fact, I keep two copies—one in the bag, one in my human's pack. Don't leave home without it.

With a little planning, a small dog can travel in the cabin, if not fly first class. You might be stuck with under-seat status, but still, it's better than cargo. As I always say, it's much better to be wearing Prada than to be stacked under it. In addition, there are so many lovely carriers out there that you and your biped will be able to shop till you drop. But in general, you big-boned dogs are out of luck. You'll be traveling cargo, I'm sorry to say. At the mercy of the baggage handlers. Wheeled around from place to place in an "airline approved" traveling crate. (To which, I needn't add, every kind of i.d. has been attached, of course). Your person, naturally, will never, ever let you fly in extremes of heat or cold, lest you be left sitting out on the tarmac, frying or freezing. Still, even in the most optimum situations—direct, non-stop flights in moderate weather (and please, no turbulence between here and there) it can pluck your last nerve. Which is why I prefer private planes. So much better for everyone, don't you agree?

...A travel bag can be a wonderful way to express a whimsical personality.

99

Showing Off
and Hooking Up

pedigree or wannabe

You're a show dog? Snaps to you. And I won't even tease you about your ridiculous name. I know it's not your real one. After all, I have one myself. But we need to talk dog shows.

Let's begin with my favorite. Yes! Yes! Yes! The Westminster Kennel Club Dog Show at Madison Square Garden. The biggest dog show in the country. One of the last remaining benched shows. Oh, don't worry, when a dog has been benched, she's still a player. A benched show is simply a show where the dogs who are competing must remain at the show and in view of the public during the day of their event. It's PR, darling, good for the American Kennel Club, and an excellent chance for humans who fancy a particular dog to go and meet the breed in person and ask (one hopes) intelligent and searching questions of breeders who (one also hopes) are scrupulous and honest enough to give detailed and unflinching answers.

Deep breath. Where was I? Oh, yes. True confessions here. I can't get in to the big show. I'm registered (for whatever that is worth, since I never intend to have puppies), but I'm just not center ring material. Boo hoo. As if I wouldn't rather be at home watching it on TV with my person, making rude remarks about what the humans are wearing.

Here's a big fashion tip, ladies and gentlemen: Fur coats at a dog show are not a good choice.

...Fur coats on humans are so Neanderthal.

I've never really understood the relationship humans have to wearing dead animal skins below the Arctic circle, but maybe it is akin to the enjoyment we dogs derive from a really good roll in something dead out in the woods. The smell, human olfactory deficiencies to the contrary, is quite divine, provided one does not over-indulge. And if you're being considerate, avoid the perfume. The dogs are going to be overwhelmed enough without the perfume assault tactic.

As to the dogs at the show, once again, poodles are made into topiary. Snicker, snicker. And don't get me started about the barbarous clipping of tails and ears. It makes those parts of me just fold up thinking about it. Oh am I soap-boxing again? Well, let me curb myself. I must step back and admit: this big American Dog Show is fun. Strolling the benching area near the ring, you will find people who look like their dogs; dogs who look like their people; dogs who are gazing with great, polite longing at the passing fur coats; dogs meeting and greeting; dogs of every size, shape, and nature. Every one of the dogs and most of the humans are delightful ambassadors for the canine world. And the show ring! Well, during the day it resembles a six or seven or eight ring circus. Each ring is presided over by a judge. Into each ring, at regular intervals, parade particular breeds.

AND THE SHOW RING! WELL, DURING THE DAY IT RESEMBLES A SIX OR SEVEN OR EIGHT RING CIRCUS.

Who knew how many people were enamored of affenpinschers? Who didn't know how many people had gone golden retriever? How the judge makes a decision amid that plethora of pups and people is anybody's guess. But at the end of the day, all the breeds who've strutted their stuff have had one best of breed chosen, along with one best of opposite sex (the gender that didn't win BOB). Those BOBs will be shown on the final night, going nose to nose first against all the other dogs in their particular groups (Seven groups in all, if you must know, divided somewhat logically and officially known as the Sporting Group, the Hound Group, the Working Group, the Terrier Group, the Toy Group, the Non-Sporting Group and the Herding Group. Yes, Terriers and Herding Dogs both are working dogs, but then every mother is a working mother, so just let it go, okay?) and then throwing it down with the best dog or bitch from each group. Is there a bias among the judges toward topiary? Some people think so. I only mention it in passing.

The big night is truly spectacular.

Canine royalty is on show, and even the human stars who come in hopes of small screen face time and are in fact interviewed to give "human" interest to the dog story cannot shine as our four footed luminaries do.

Which goes a long way toward explaining just why some of the handlers wear what they wear. Do they honestly believe sequins are going to make their dachshund look more dashing to the judge? Or that we can overlook the unfortunate combination of practical sneakers and long silky skirt? Well, you be the judge of that.

...As dog show attire goes, sequins and sneakers simply do not mix. Pearls are the way to go. Always tasteful. So Jackie-O!

But wait. We've come to the big moment. Seven dogs remain, one from each group. The judge (who, I have observed, is always elegantly dressed and nicely pulled together, whether male or female) commands each dog to come forward. She watches the dog walk up and back. She pats the dog down, making sure all parts are where they should be. Finally, she walks up and down the rows of dogs. She pauses, considers, walks on. The dogs stand at attention, also known as stacking.

Oooh, look she's checking out the Maltese that won the toy group. Cheers from the Maltese fan club.

"Pick me, pick me, pick me," say the eyes of the handlers. "Got a treat, got a treat, got a treat?" say the eyes of their dogs. She takes another close look at the wire fox terrier who won the terrier group. I cheer on principal. Then pauses, sigh, before a large, beige topiary poodle. Who do you think she will pick?

Well. It takes all kinds to make a dog show.

...Nip tuck

Dating, Mating and Procreating

As you may have observed, dogs and humans hook up in quite different ways. But the results are often the same. Let's talk puppies once more. And if we talk puppies, we must use the "S" word and the "N" word: spay and neuter.

Yes, I know, you were a puppy once yourself. Yes, I know, nothing is cuter then your own little quadruped flesh and blood. But the sad truth is, there are more than enough puppies to go around. Too many puppies to grow up and become dogs with badly trained people who decide not to keep them.

So you've been spayed, right? Or neutered? Oooh, look. I can just imagine the male humans clamping their knees together. They just take it so personally, don't they? And we don't even notice.

Still, puppies happen. How do you think all the dogs at the American Kennel Club dog shows got there? Not to mention the non-AKC registered but still highly desirable mixed breeds.

Of course, in my day, dogs of any mixed heritage were known as mutts. Though the term was often softened with the addition of the word "lovable," a mutt was still somehow viewed as second-rate. But thankfully times have changed and, we have become more socially conscious, so it is now quite chic to be descended from parents of different breeds—a fact

that dogs have known all along. I am, of course, too well bred, in the social graces sense, to point out the obvious hilarity of the breed names with which some of our dear brethren are now saddled as a result of these canine social parings. I leave that to you, dear reader. But really...Cockapoo? Labradoodle? Schnoodle? Saint Berdoodle? How about a bull terrier and shih tzu? Oh, no you don't.

...The scruffy look is IN.

But these are all designer dogs, darling. And like all designer desirables of the moment, priced for the designer market. Who knew?

Dog Breed Mathematics

Cocker Spaniel + Poodle = Cockapoo

Labrador + Poodle = Labradoodle

Schnauzer + Poodle = Schnoodle

Doberman + Standard Poodle = Doodleman Pinscher

...Pure breeds are SO overrated.

Those of us who've had parents from different groups have always just called ourselves cross-breeds. Not to mention those other meetings between nice bitches of no particular breed and strangers in the night.

Mutts. Mixed breeds. And every one with the potential to be a petrosexual if you ask *moi*. Which just proves that perfect dogs come in all shapes and sizes, and from everywhere.

Oh, so serious of me, but I'll say it. If your person starts to think about adding another dog (or, alright, another cat) to your little ménage, try to guide him toward a rescue organization, shelter, or breeder with a good reputation. So many of my dear, dear friends come from rescue organizations.

Even the cat, quite a tolerable cat, with whom I share my space, came from a rescue. And without the rescue programs where would they be? One shudders to think. After all, life isn't just a dog show. Is it?

...From a caterpillar into a butterfly

Conclusion:
You like me, you really like me.

A Petrosexual Is Born

Look at you. Elegant. Sophisticated. Tastefully attired in a natty collar that has a matching leash neatly hung up somewhere nearby. Maybe you didn't get such an easy start in life, but look at you now. You eat leftovers from the best restaurants. You walk in the best parks. You can handle a cat. Your owner is polite and well behaved. Luck? Chance? *Au contraire.*

From the moment you went to the trouble of making sure your person was the right match for the kind of dog you are, you were making your own luck. That early training didn't hurt. You had him housetrained and loving it in no time. You travel everywhere

together. You've barked encouragement at the softball league games in the park. You've even been to her office on those weekends when she had to work. And he says when he goes out on his own, you're coming to the office every day. Look around. Thanks to you, his neighborhood is not just some place he's passing through. He knows it well, by dawn and by dusk. She's met people in the park that she might never have known. When he walks down the street, people stop to talk to him—why? Because he's your "dad." Dare I say it? You've grown up together. He might still be a member of the girlfriend of the week club, but from you, he's learned commitment and patience. Acquired a bit better fashion sense. Through you, he might even meet a nice female biped and engage in that human ritual, marriage. It seems to make them happy, and you do like for them to be happy. Am I getting sentimental? 'Fraid so.

Still, you've become the dog you were meant to be. With a little more work, he'll be quite the human. And you'll always be together. Oh, dab a tear from my eye. Who's responsible for all this delight? Well, me, in part, naturally. But take a look in the mirror. Someone else had quite a paw in it, too.

Who's that delightful creature? That warm and wise canine? That noble being? Well, who do you think? **You.**

Photo Credits

7; 9 Chesapeake Bay Retriever, pug; 13 Chow Chow; 14 Cavalier King Charles Spaniel; 15; 25 Hungarian greyhound; 27; 36 Staffordshire Bull Terrier; 48; 49; 50; 53; 56; 57; 59; 61; 62; 63; 64; 65 Bull Terrier; 66 Boston Terrier; 68; 71; 72; 74; 75; 79; 81; 82; 87; 92 Chihuahua; 97; 102; 103; 105; 109 © Quarto Publishing

Copyright page (dog in leis) Comstock Images/Getty Images; 14 (nose) The Image Bank/Getty Images; 25 (dalmatian) Photographer's Choice/Getty Images; 33 (tennis balls) Stone/Getty Images, (dog with stick) The Image Bank/Getty Images; 35 Stone/Getty Images; 37 The Image Bank/Getty Images; 38 Stone/Getty Images; 39 Taxi/Getty Images; 65 (dog on leash) Brand X Pictures/Getty Images; 70 (dog in sunglasses) Stone/Getty Images; 85 Stone/Getty Images; 88 Taxi/Getty Images; 89 Stone/Getty Images; 91 Stone/Getty Images; 93 Stone/Getty Images; 95 The Image Bank/Getty Images; 96 Stone/Getty Images

13 head close-up; 17; 24; 28; 30; 34; 43 dog in Santa hat; 54; 55; 73; 83; 106; 107; 108 © Jane Burton/Warren Photographic

36 dog with stick; 47; 67; 70 black dog in field; 76; 77 © Horsepix

20 bulldog on checkered bed; 22: Photo courtesy of Postmodern Pets, Inc.—www.postmodernpets.com

41, 42 two dogs in collared shirts; 46; 51 dog in Superstar sweater; 98 two dogs in black bag: Photos courtesy of Kwigy-Bo Inc—Luxuries for Dogs

19, 80, 111: Photos courtesy of Glamour Dog. Glamour Dog is a registered trademark of Casey Witcher dba Glamour Dog

20 dog on bone bed: photo Stephanie Son/The Ritzy Rover; 23 doghouse: photo La Petite Maison/The Ritzy Rover; 29 plate of treats: photo Michelle Pellette/The Ritzy Rover; 45 feather collar: Prissy Paws/The Ritzy Rover; 98 white dogs in gray bag: photo Stephanie Son/The Ritzy Rover; 99 photo: World According to Jess/The Ritzy Rover
The Ritzy Rover/Prissy Paws

32: Photo courtesy of Betty Russell Ojakli

All other photos: Don Ayres © Walter Foster Publishing dba Paint Chip Productions

Where to Shop

Diamond Dogs (U.K.) Limited
www.diamonddogs.us

Glamour Dog
www.glamourdog.com

Kwigy-bo
www.kwigy-bo.com

Molly Marie's Pretties of Las Vegas
www.mollymariespretties.homestead.com

Postmodern Pets
www.postmodernpets.com

The Ritzy Rover Pet Boutique
www.theritzyrover.com

Trinitee's Closet
www.triniteescloset.com

...High maintenance dahling, but worth it.

Acknowledgments

Products

Front Cover: Papillon model, Jazzy, CH Amour's Sweet Jazzy, Amour Papillons on Botanical Green Sofa, courtesy of The Ritzy Rover Pet Boutique.

Saluki model, Wyatte, Burydown Wyatte, wearing Destinee's Dream coat, courtesy of Trinitee's Closet.

Back Cover: Weimaraner model, Jewel, CH Silverado Ingenue, wearing Pillow Talk coat, courtesy of Trinitee's Closet.

Title Page: (Left) Karmen, Whippet model; Bohemian Groove bed, courtesy of The Ritzy Rover Pet Boutique; Swarovski Crystal collar by Diamond Dogs (U.K.) Limited. (Right) Slim, Whippet model; Retro Flower coat, courtesy of The Ritzy Rover Pet Boutique.

Contents Page: Robbie, Cavalier King Charles Spaniel model; Mr. Wall Street coat, courtesy of Trinitee's Closet.

4: Karmen, Whippet model; Swarovski Crystal collar by Diamond Dogs (U.K.) Limited.

5: Robbie, Cavalier King Charles Spaniel model.

10: JR, Italian Greyhound model.

11: Buster, Boxer model.

18: Jazzy, Papillon model; Botanical Green Sofa, courtesy of The Ritzy Rover Pet Boutique.

19: Fife, Yorkshire Terrier model; Feathered Canopy bed courtesy of GlamourDog; pink bow with Swarovski Crystal Heart, courtesy of Molly Marie's Pretties of Las Vegas.

20: (Top) Checker Dog Bed courtesy of Postmodern Pets Inc.; (Bottom) Sweater and Boney Rug courtesy of The Ritzy Rover Pet Boutique.

21: Mahogany Sleigh Bed and Pretty in Pink Dress courtesy of GlamourDog.

22: All beds courtesy of Postmodern Pets, Inc.

23: La Petite Maison dog house available from The Ritzy Rover Pet Boutique.

29: Little Peanut Butter Biscuits available from The Ritzy Rover Pet Boutique.

32: Betty, Jack Russell model.

41: Sweaters from Kwigy-bo.

42: Jewel, Weimaraner model; Pillow Talk coat, courtesy of Trinitee's Closet. Collared shirts from Kwigy-bo.

43: Jewel and Trinitee, Weimaraner models.

44: Trinitee, Weimaraner model.

45: Trinitee, Weimaraner model; custom made, velvet, rhinestone and lace collar, courtesy of The Ritzy Rover Pet Boutique; Glamarama Couture collar, courtesy of The Ritzy Rover Pet Boutique.

46: Robe from Kwigy-bo.

51: (Right) Sweater from Kwigy-bo; (Left) JR, Italian Greyhound model, wearing Mocha Dot coat, courtesy of The Ritzy Rover Pet Boutique.

58: Jazzy, Papillon model.

69: Wyatte, Saluki model.

80: Celebrity Dog Bed from GlamourDog.

84: Skyla, baby model; Maka, Labrador Retriever model.

98: (Left) Dual Classic Bag from The Ritzy Rover Pet Boutique; (Right) Emily Bag from Kwigy-bo.

99: Pampered Puppy Carrier from The Ritzy Rover Pet Boutique.

104: Wyatte, Saluki model; Destinee's Dream coat, courtesy of Trinitee's Closet.

109: Jazzy, Papillon model.

110: Carmen, Whippet model; Tapered Random Swarovski Crystal collar by Diamond Dogs (U.K.) Limited.

Backmatter: Shimmering Pink Mink Bed from GlamourDog.

Models

Whippet models courtesy of Crestfield Whippets, Herb and Martha Fielder, Napa, CA. CH Crestfield That Girl "Marlo" and her daughter Crestfield Catch A Star "Slim". Boxer model, Buster, courtesy of the Miles family. RMiles1600@yahoo.co.jp

Yorkshire Terrier model courtesy of Patricia Hamer, San Francisco, CA. Robtell Kingdom of Fife, Fife.

Whippet models courtesy of Darcey Hopkins, Carmichael, CA. it_be_cheez@yahoo.com

Karmen, Windy Days Down in Jamaica, Casey, Elandans Moonshadow

Boston Terrier model, Tiger, Blossom's Go Get 'Em Tiger, courtesy of Kristina Leslie, Vacaville, CA.

Boxer model, Tai Tai, courtesy of Jenn Nicoson, Lower Lake, CA.

Cavalier King Charles Spaniel model courtesy of Rambler Dalmatians & Cavaliers, Joanne Nash & Jan Rowley: CH Rambler Robin Hood, CGC, Robbie.

Saluki model "Wyatte" aka Burydown Wyatte, JC, courtesy of Shelby Salukis. Shelby421@aol.com.

Italian Greyhound models courtesy of Westwind Italian Greyhounds, Audrey Sutton, Saratoga, CA. Westwind Justinian Royal, Westwind La Principessa

Papillon models are by Amour Papillons, Northern California. Loved, owned, shown and bred by Constance A. Wardell and Dr. Jonathan W. Wardell of Northern California. Papillonprincess@sbcglobal.net

CH Amour's Nobel Prize (red and white papillon) also known as "Ginger" by her loved ones.

CH Amour's Sweet Jazzy (black and white papillon) also known as "Jazzy" by her loved ones.

Weimaraner models courtesy of Silverado Weimaraners, Michael Ayers & Shiffra Steele, Middletown, CA. www.grayghost.org

Jewel, CH Silverado Ingenue

Trinitee, CH Silverado Destinee's Child NSD, CGC

Jack Russell model courtesy of Sumya Ojakli. Betty

...Pretentious? Yes. Fabulous? Absolutely!